Money and Common Sense

Tammy Nelson

Money and Common Sense

Author: Tammy Nelson

Images: Tammy Nelson
&
G. and Co. Design

This book was designed to be a reference resource only. The information presented in this book was created in order to assist you in utilizing common sense in making financial decisions. It is by no way intended as a replacement for any advice you may receive from a professional financial advisor or financial planner. Any financial investments can have potential risks. The author and publisher are not responsible in any manner for profits or losses that you, the reader may incur as a result of reading this book.

Internet search references and terms were accurate at the time this book was published.

© 2016 Tammy Nelson

This book can be purchased for educational and business purposes, book clubs, book groups, or sales promotional use. Electronic books can be purchased online. For more information on book purchases or requesting a Money and Common Sense Seminar, please write T. Nelson, Requests Dept., P.O. Box 23, Monroeville, PA 15146 or email moneyandcommonsense@gmail.com .

This book is recommended for people who want to learn how to manage their money using common sense and simple strategies.

Contents

Introduction

Money doesn't grow on trees is a true cliché. If it did, everyone would be rich. However, this book is designed to help you save more of the money you have earned.

This book provides strategies that will enable you to earn money. It will cleverly help you save instantaneously on your purchases and avoid get rich quick schemes. It will show you what to ask for when shopping and spending for your needs. It will help you prevent the destruction of your budget during your shopping excursions. Also, this book exposes you to credit score basics, how to maneuver around the credit card trap, when and why buy a warranty, investing ideas, and where to donate or tithe.

If you are thirteen years old or one hundred thirteen years old, you will be able to read this book and ascertain the knowledge and skills to be successful with your money. It is relatively, quite that simple, but you must adhere to following the strategies presented in this book with common sense. You must put in the time to use the strategies, and you will financially reap the benefits by having more money staying in your pocket or bank account.

Life is short; no one wants to be upset and frustrated about his or her finances all of the time. Therefore, this book is designed to help alleviate this type of stress. You can feel much happier and less worried when you know you are managing your money with common sense.

I.   Earn Income

Chapter 1
Get and Keep a Job

First and foremost, unless you are already a multi-millionaire, this book is going to assist you in recognizing an important part of your life. This important part is called your job. Why is it so important? It is important because it's usually your main source of <mark>income</mark> or money flowing into your pocket and household. You can use the money you have earned to save, spend, invest, and donate.

If you are unemployed, you will need to find a suitable job that will utilize your skills. If there are no suitable jobs available, you may have to select from whatever jobs are available. You have alternative choices as well. You can choose to go back to school to train for a new profession, or you can choose to create your own legal business by providing a service like landscaping, snow removal, babysitting/childcare.

Once you have your job, you need to keep your job by providing a stellar work performance. In order to promote your business's good reputation, you must supply quality products and superior services. News of your boss's excellent evaluations or customers' highly favorable references will quickly spread like a wild fire.

Once you are hired, you need to keep your job by arriving 10 to 15 minutes early, leaving on time, and don't sneak out early. Have a pleasant attitude and leave your personal problems at home. No one wants to work with a grumpy, sarcastic, person with a poor attitude. Don't miss too many days; refer to your company's absenteeism policy concerning missing work. If you own your own business, don't cancel appointments with your business clients. Also, make sure you tidy up your work environment before you leave for the day. <u>Be excellent, no matter if you are working a job or are running your own business.</u> Provide quality goods and services at a fair price in order to obtain new and repeat customers. These are solid ways to keep a job once you get one or to keep your business running once it is established.

Chapter 2
Get Rich Quick Schemes

Have you ever experienced a situation where you received an email to work from home and make thousands of dollars, or you've won a sweepstakes or contest you have never heard of. Friends want you to join a group to sell spices, prepaid vacations, or plastic products through a pyramid format. Some of these schemes require you to invest large sums of money in order to get started. You may not ever recoup your investment. Other schemes will want you to buy large quantities of their inventory to sell, and the items may not sell as quickly as explained in their sales' pitches. More sinister schemes will encourage you to wire money to third party businesses where fraudulent thieves will take your money. Therefore, get rich quick schemes have a strong potential to lead you to the poor house quickly.

There are times when you can stumble upon an easy job where people are willing to pay $40 or $50 for you to cut their lawns. If you do five lawns in a day, you may make $200 a day. That's a good payment for one day's worth of work.

Let's look at get rich quick and ==pyramid schemes==. You have to realize, if you are on the top of the pyramid, you will receive a portion of everyone's profits. When you start on the entry or bottom level, you will have to recruit more people and invest more money in order to ascend your way to the top. It may take a lot of time, recruits, and investments of your own money to succeed in a get rich quick scheme.

To put it in plain English, you can't get something for nothing. Don't fall for get rich quick or pyramid schemes.

II.   Saving

Chapter 3
Instant Savings and a Budget

The word, "Save" can have two meanings. First, it can mean to reduce the price you pay for an item, or in other words, it's an instant savings. The second meaning is to create and store away a surplus of cash for use at a later date. Read on for more ways to save!

Coupons are not a Secret. Use them!

One of the easiest ways to save money is by using coupons. It's no secret. They come in the mail in some areas. In other areas you have to make an investment in purchasing a Sunday paper. Coupons can be obtained from online coupon sites, through coupon apps, or by purchasing a coupon book. Visit store websites and click on their savings/coupon links. For instant coupons you can also sign up for store savings cards and e-coupon email lists. Check the bottoms and backs of store receipts for coupons or for surveys you can complete in order to receive a coupon for a free item or a percentage discount on your next purchase. Don't forget to check your junk mail for coupons and offers.

You can join an extreme coupon group or attend an extreme couponing class in order to learn the art of extreme couponing. Extreme couponing will tremendously lower your weekly shopping bills.

Also, find stores that double or stack coupons for extra savings. Some stores even will text you information about coupons and savings. Finally, watch TV commercials, search websites, and view the local paper ads to monitor sales, and obtain special limited time paper coupons. There are rebate websites and apps that will pay you back a percentage of your spending at certain stores.

Most importantly, you can do an Internet search for the latest, greatest, popular coupon web sites, coupon clubs, rebate websites, and apps. I would do a monthly search because new sites and apps are created every day. That is why I am not recommending any website or app today that could be passé in the near future.

Buy It. Pay It. Save It. It's Magic!

There are times when you may be able to save 20% or more off of the original or sale price if you charge it on the store credit/charge card in your first transaction. Then pay your bill off right away in a second transaction. This way your credit/charge card will have a zero balance because you pay the amount charged off immediately. I am not suggesting you use it and carry a balance. That is why you have to be diligent and pay the charged amount off instantaneously. Why? Your ultimate goal is to save money and eventually live debt free without any credit/charge card balances.

Search for Coupon Codes Before You Make an Online Purchase

You can find some awesome deals when you shop online. Even better, you can do a search for coupon codes for the store you are purchasing items from.

What are coupon codes? Coupon codes are a series of numbers, letters, or numbers and letters that you can use to apply to your online order to save. Sometimes the savings are a percentage off of your purchase price. Other times you may receive free shipping or earn a free gift.

My last purchase online I found a coupon code for 12% off of my order of $359.99. The coupon subtracted $43.20 off of the purchase price. I paid only $316.79. I can now put that $43.20 towards my savings, or I can put that money towards this week's grocery bill.

Online Groups, Scan for Savings, and Apps

There are a variety of online groups, apps, and blogs where you sign up to become a member and pre-purchase goods and services at steep discounts. You will be emailed or enabled to print out a confirmation certificate, receipt, or coupon that confirms your purchase. In most cases, you must use it before the expiration date.

If you are making a purchase at a big box store that price matches the advertised prices of their competitors, you will need the competitors' advertisements, your smart cell phone, and a scanning app. You can show the cashier or customer service representative a competitor's advertisement paper or web advertisement that includes the better price you would like to pay for that item. Also, there are several barcode and QR Code scanning apps. These apps allow you to scan a product's bar code. The product's information (item name and competitive vendor prices) will pop up. Then you can show the cashier the competitive/comparative price. The cashier will verify the price, and he or she will have to match the lowest fair competitor's price. Unfortunately many stores will not honor online auction prices. However, you will put the power of price matching right at your fingertips.

If you don't have a smart phone, any store that price matches should also accept paper advertisements as well. The perk of using the scanner app is that the scanner may find stores that may not be near you. These stores may have much cheaper prices than the local paper ads.

There are also apps that will help you price compare and retrieve any money you may have overpaid for items. There are other apps that will send you rebates for your purchases, and some apps will pay you to shop or just locate particular items. Do an app search in order to find the apps that will work best for you.

Use Your Membership Benefits!

Most union memberships have extra perks, the benefits of savings! Check with your union to see if they have discount information sheets or brochures on where and how much you can save.

Also, some auto clubs may have discounts. Just show your membership card at restaurants, shoe stores, and other service providers. Again, check with your auto club's benefits' brochure to see where, when, and how much you can save.

Definitely, if you are a senior citizen 55 years of age or older, ask for a senior discount. Some places honor senior citizens at age 55; other places honor senior citizens at age 65. You may have to present a valid identification card. Then simply enjoy your discount.

Sales

First, every time there is a sale you don't have to buy something. A sale needs to be investigated and compared to prices of that same item online and in other stores before you can shout, "I've found a bargain!!!"

If you are interested in purchasing anything from clothing to a major appliance, visit the store and online to do your homework. Check the original/off-sale price. Then calculate the sales price to ensure there is a savings. If you see a sign that says 20% off, calculate 20% off of the original price. Why? You want to make sure the store has calculated the savings correctly.

Make a comparison list of stores, prices, and sale prices. While making your purchase, scan the barcodes to see if a local store may have the exact item or a comparable item for a cheaper price.

Remember to review your daily newspaper. There may be extra savings coupons on top of the sales.

Follow the holiday sales. Some holiday sales are better than others. For example, you can find bargains for men around Father's Day and deals for women around Mother's Day. Black Friday has just about the best sales if you plan your shopping right. I had a budget of $600 and purchased everything I needed for my family of four, my parents, and a family friend. In actuality, I spent $594.00. I was $6 under budget.

Finally, buy off-season for the best deals and bargains. I have purchased $390 leather, designer boots for $120 in the spring. That was almost a 70% savings. In other words, I had $270 to save or spend towards my household bills.

Perks and Points for Gas

A wonderful way to save money is by signing up for gas pump perks or pump points. You can go to a store that offers it and sign up for a gas pump perk/point card. It works when you buy groceries and products such as gift cards and quick cooked foods. For each purchase a certain amount or percentage of your total purchase will go towards your pump perks or points. For example, you will receive 5 cents off per gallon for every $25 spent. Especially around the holidays, your gas perks and points will add up quickly.

I have a personal testimony. When I needed a new dryer, I purchased $550 worth of gift cards from my pump perks store where I received $1.10 off per gallon of gas. I filled my SUV up and took gas cans to fill up as well. It was a nice kickback of cash and gas especially when I had to make a major purchase.

Real Freebies!

There are times when you will encounter things that are free. For example, if you attend a car show, a motor company may give you a free t-shirt if you sign up for their mailing list, or they may give you a free gift card to take a test drive. These items are free, but you may have to put up with annoying emails, take a test drive, or put up with pesky phone calls from the salespeople of the motor company. If you are willing to do that, then enjoy your free t-shirt or gift cards.

Keep Receipts

Every time you make a purchase immediately review your receipt for price errors. Please do this before you leave the store! Finding a mistake at the store can easily be corrected. Finding a mistake at home will cause you to make a trip back to the store to correct the receipt's error.

Always keep receipts until the date on it says that the items are non-returnable. Why? For instance, if the item is a purse and the seams start to tear, then take the purse, the receipt, and return or exchange it.

Finally, to help with organization, buy an accordion file folder to keep receipts filed by general purchases, purchases with warranties, and receipts for tax purposes. Keeping everything in one, neat place will help you stay organized. It will also make life easier during tax time.

Balance Your Checkbook and Have a Budget

One final point about saving is to strategically plan your spending. Create a budget because a budget is imperative. Why? A budget concentrates your finances on spending for your needs. It doesn't matter how much you save on sale items if you blow your budget in the process it's not worth it.

How does a budget help you save? It allows you to view how much money you earn and subtract the costs of your needs in order to see how much money is left for saving, investing, and donating. Then if there is any money left once you have saved, invested, and donated, then you can purchase something you want or choose to add this additional amount to your savings account.

Sample budgets are located in the appendix of the book. Choose one and use it.

Balancing your checkbook is a visual way to instantly keep track of your actual spending. There are apps for balancing your checkbook, and your bank may utilize an online checkbook program as well. You will find that balancing your checkbook is very simple to do. However, in this book, I will concentrate on balancing a paper checkbook.

First, write down the current balance or the amount of money you have in your checking account onto the backside of a deposit ticket in the back section of your checkbook. If you do not have deposit tickets, you may want to use the back cover of your checkbook to balance your checkbook. You can also use a ledger/register or a notebook to do this as well, but the inside of your checkbook seems to work best.

Next, whenever you write a check, or make a purchase on your checking account's debit card, and pay bills that you have automatically deducted or automatically drafted from your account every month, subtract those amounts from your balance. Also, remember to deduct any monthly reoccurring bank fees. The new amount or the difference is your new balance or what you have in your checking account. Repeat this process every time you write a check or use your debit card. This way you will know what your account's balance is before you spend any more money.

The awesome thing about this is that it reflects checks that companies or people may not have cashed immediately. In reality it may take 2 or more days before a check becomes deducted from your account. You can accidentally forget that you wrote the check and spend that money, and when the check comes in you are either short or could possibly overdraw your account.

No one wants to overdraw an account. There are fees of $25 or more for each check that comes into an overdrawn account.

Below is a sample ledger/register photograph.

	7-1	Paycheck		700
Check 101	7-2	Rent		-350
				350
Online Pay	7-5	Electric Bill		-100
				250
Debit	7-7	Food / Groceries		-100
				150
Check 102	7-10	Tithe		-70
				80
Debit	7-12	Bus Pass		-40
		Spending Money until Pay day		40
		Pay Day (7-15)		

A sample budget is included on the next page. There are also two budget worksheets included in the appendix of this book.

A Sample Budget

Name of Bills	Payment Amount	Due Date	Comments
Rent or Mortgage	$550	1st	
Electric	$65	1st	
Gas	$50	1st	
Cell &/or Home Phone	$30	Card refill	Every 90 days
Water/Sewer	$45	15th	
Cable or Satellite TV Subscriptions	$70	15th	
Food & Lunches	$70	monthly	Ongoing
Medicine	$10	1st	
Entertainment	$50	As needed	Ongoing
Gas/Bus Pass/Ride Share Fees	$50		
Child Care	$300	1st	
Clothing	$40	As needed	Ongoing
Insurance (auto, home/renters, life, health)	$125	15th	
Credit Card or Charge Accounts			
1.Charge A Mania Credit Card	$50	15th	
2.			
3.			
4.			
Loan Payments			
1.Hoopty Rides Car Loan	$150	15th	
2.			
3.			
Church/Charity Donations	$200	1st	
Miscellaneous/Unexpected	$10	As needed	Ongoing
Savings	$50	15th	
Investments	$50	15th	
Total Expenses Per Month	$1965		
Actual Take Home Pay Per Month	$2000		
Subtract Total Expenses from Actual Take Home Pay = Net (what you have left over). Fill Net in next box.	$2000 -$1965 Net= $35		
The goal is to have some money left over.	$35 left over		

Chapter 4
Know What to Ask For

There are times when you go to a restaurant for take-out, and you pay for your food. You take your bagged food order and leave.

Well, slow down partner! Always ask for these items: paper plates, napkins, plastic cutlery, straws, and sauce. These items should be free with the purchase of your meal. Even if you don't use the items right then, you may need them the next day if you have leftovers.

Here is how to get a free salad… If you are ordering a take-out hoagie or submarine sandwich, ask for your veggie toppings to be put into separate plastic baggies or containers on the side. Why? Unless you have to have all of your veggies placed on your sandwich, the separated veggies can be used partly on the sandwich, and the rest of the remaining veggies can be used to make a salad.

Remember ask for salad dressings and anything else free that you are entitled to. Whatever free items you don't use, store them in the fridge and use them later.

In addition to that, whether you are in a restaurant or a store ask the cashier if there are any extra discounts, specials, or percentages off of your total purchase for today. This will allow the cashier to reveal any club card savings or recommend items that may be similar in the clearance areas.

Sometimes you need to buy items in bulk or multiple items of one product at one time. Always ask the cashier or store manager if he or she can provide a discount.

If you are purchasing an article of clothing and the clothing is either missing a button or has some defect, ask for a discount or a price adjustment. The normal discount ranges between 5% and 10%.

Remember, in many circumstances, you must ask for the discounts, special savings, and price adjustments available. Many cashiers won't readily volunteer this information

Chapter 5
Bank Accounts or the Coffee Can

After you have saved money on your shopping experiences, what do you do with the money you didn't spend? Simply, if you have more than five dollars in cash, deposit it into a savings account or a money market account. The good thing about bank accounts or money market accounts is that your savings will earn a small percent of interest.

If you have saved $4.99 or less in spare change, deposit that money into a coffee can or piggy bank. The goal of this type of savings is to build a liquid emergency fund. You can keep depositing money into the can until it's full and take it to a bank's coin counter where it won't collect fees. The coin counter will provide you with a cashable receipt for the money. Then you can put any amounts over $5.00 into your savings account. Again, any amounts less than $5.00 can be kept at home and used as liquid cash for days when you are short a dollar for lunch money or bus fare. This is a great way to pay for the unexpected petty cash emergencies.

Direct Deposit is a Great Way to Automatically Save

If your employer has automatic, direct deposit, you can select to have most of your paycheck directly deposited into your checking account and have a minimum of 10% of your pay deposited directly into your savings account. This way you don't even touch the money before it is safely sent to your savings.

Many people enjoy the perks of saving this way. Saving in this manner allows you to only use the money in the checking account while the money in the savings account remains to grow if you don't touch it.

III.   When to Spend

Chapter 6
Spend for Your Needs

When you have to spend money, spend it on your needs and not your wants. A <mark>need</mark> is something basic you are required to have in order to survive or function appropriately. Examples are basic food, clothing, transportation, and shelter. <mark>Wants</mark> are the more extravagant version of your need. For instance, you need an affordable car, but you want the pricey, sports car.

Let's be realistic, there are times when you are tempted to purchase more extravagant necessities like dining out at a four star restaurant, purchasing expensive designer clothing or purses, stepping up to an expensive luxury car, and buying a mini-mansion. Don't do it unless you have a large enough income to afford such purchases. Also, only purchase these items if the purchases do not negatively affect your budget by taking money away from your bill payments.

Here is why you should spend for your basic needs and not for luxury items. It's a word called <mark>depreciation</mark>. When you buy a brand new car, especially a luxury car, you will learn that right after you drive it off the lot, it's value can decrease around $3,000 or more in most cases. That's a clear example of depreciation. Why? Once you buy the car; you are the owner. It is will be considered a used car if you had to trade it in.

Used designer purses and clothing sell for a fraction of their original prices on used clothing and auction sites. If the housing market conditions are not right, you could pay a high price for a mini-mansion. The housing market could correct itself, and the value of the mini-mansion may be a lot less than what you paid for it. If you would try to sell it in a corrected housing market, you may not sell it for what you originally paid for it. Also, eating an expensive meal in a fancy restaurant is nice for special occasions, but unless you are a millionaire, expensive nightly dinners at fancy restaurants should not be in your budget.

Always think twice when spending. Ask yourself, "Is this a need or a want?"

If it is a need and you can afford it, spend the money to purchase it as long as it fits into your budget. If it is a want that you know you really can't afford, don't bust your budget. Go for an affordable option to satisfy your need.

Cell Phones

If your smart cell phone bill is almost as much or more than your car insurance payment, then you need to trade down to a lower costing cell phone once your contract is over. Sometimes, a few cell phone carriers will buy you out of your contract and give you a better deal on a lower priced phone and maybe allow you to enroll into a lower month to month non-contract agreement. I would suggest shop around for the best non-contract cell phone and payment options.

I like the prepaid wireless cell phones. Some plans will allow you to purchase a certain amount of minutes, and the minutes are good for 90 days or until you use all of your minutes. These minute cell phones can really save you lots of money if you are not wasteful and use your minutes with common sense.

Remember, in today's high tech world a cell phone is a need. However, don't over burden your budget with a pricey cell phone plan unless your budget allows you to do so. Therefore, prepaid wireless and non-contract cell phones can be an affordable option of having a cell phone without breaking your budget.

Chapter 7
Credit Score Basics

Your <mark>credit score</mark> is a number assigned to you that companies access when you apply for a mortgage, car loan, or other types of credit. Your credit score can be bolstered by paying your bills on time, not opening tons of new credit cards, using only 10-30% of your available credit, and not canceling credit cards that you barely use. Also, your credit score is affected by your debt to income ratio as well.

Why is your credit score so important? It determines the type of interest rates for your loans. It can also determine whether a mortgage company will underwrite your mortgage for your home purchase. People who have high credit scores usually are able to receive the 0% interest on a car loan. People with low credit scores can receive interest rates that are possibly as high as 9% or greater for a car loan.

Two people can purchase the exact same car, for the exact same price, with the exact same loan period, on the same day, from the same dealership. One person has a low credit score. He or she will receive a higher interest rate car loan and will pay more for the car over the course of the loan period. How? The monthly payment for the person with the low credit score will be greater because of the higher interest rate.

This is the perfect example why you need to keep your credit score high. A high credit score can save you a lot of money on your major purchases.

Chapter 8
The Credit Card Trap

Every time you look around there is an offer for a credit card in your email or snail mail (regular mail). Also, every time you shop in almost any store, a cashier is suggesting that you open a new credit/ charge card account. Even worse, the credit card offers are great; some credit cards offer an instant 20% off your entire purchase or 0% interest rates on balance transfers. Well, here's how to handle this situation.

As referred to in chapter 3, credit cards, especially department store credit/charge cards, can be used to discount your purchase price, and then you must pay them off immediately. Some merchants will allow you to make the purchase and seconds later pay off your purchase. This is the best method to handle department store credit cards.

The second way to handle your credit card situation is to pay off your balance monthly. Yes, pay the entire balance off, or you will be hit with a monthly interest charge. These monthly charges can be as high as 20% or more depending on your credit card terms.

Also, if you make a large purchase like furniture or appliances and you take the 24 months same as cash deal, you better pay your balance in full by the 24th month. Why? If you don't, your 25th month balance will include 24 months of built up interest. Yes, if you even owe a few dollars, you will have a new balance that includes all of the interest from the previous 24 months added to the few remaining dollars of your previous balance. In order to clear your credit card and pay your account in full, you must pay your entire account off so you can avoid accruing more interest.

For regular credit cards that can be used at any store, it's best to only use them once in a while and pay them off monthly in order to keep them open. Also, use a regular credit card in a serious emergency. For example, use it when you have an unexpected car repair that you can't pay out of your pocket. Otherwise, keep all credit cards paid in full. If you make the mistake of carrying a balance, try to pay more than the minimum payment at least 3 days before the due date. Keep making payments this way until it is paid off.

If you fall into the credit card trap and charge up big balances on multiple credit cards, the interest will cause you to give away lots of money for free. How? The interest payments will keep inflating your remaining balance. You keep giving free money to the credit card companies in the form of interest payments. Therefore, prepaid credit cards and debit cards are better. Prepaid and debit cards have a limit of money that is available in your account. Once you spend your limit, the card will decline your next purchase. Thus, there aren't any balances to pay off. Better yet, if you can pay for purchases with cash, cash is always king.

There is one more important point for this chapter. Never cosign a loan, credit cards, a mortgage, or purchases for anyone. Why? When you cosign for someone, you are accepting responsibility for the payments even if the item(s) are not for you. Cosigning means if the person misses payments or stops paying for any reason, you will assume the responsibility of making payments until the loan is paid off, or until the person who originated the loan can start paying again.

If you don't pick up the payments, you will be held responsible. The loan, mortgage, credit card companies, and/or bank will tarnish your credit score and credit history. Then when you want to purchase a major item like a car or a home, you may possibly experience the problem of being declined a loan or given an opportunity to purchase the item with a sky-high interest rate loan. Yes, when you go to get something for yourself, your cosigning for someone else has now destroyed your credit and credit history. Cosigning actually means you promised to pay when the originator of the loan could not. Now, the bank or lender is thinking you will probably not pay their loan either because of your track record with the loan that you cosigned for someone else. Yes, with technology today, you cannot escape a poor credit score and history. All lenders know about you and how you have handled your loans and the loans you have cosigned for as well.

Chapter 9
Why Buy a Warranty

Many times when you make purchases of electronics and technological items, the cashier will ask you if you would like to purchase a warranty. A <mark>warranty</mark> is an insurance policy for an item. Quite often people will decline the warranty, but there are times when buying a warranty is recommended.

For small purchases under $100.00 or if you know that you can replace the item within 1 pay period without wrecking your budget, then you don't really need a warranty. Now, if you make a major purchase over $100.00 or you know that you can't readily replace the item in 1 pay period because it will destroy your budget, then you need to buy a warranty.

Why? Consider this; you purchase a laptop for $399.00, and you travel a lot with it, or you have children using the laptop. To get your money's worth, you should purchase a 2-year extended warranty that protects against drops, damages, and power surges.

On the other hand, if you only use your laptop and it sits on a desk or table, and you don't eat near it; then you may not need a warranty. Warranties really protect when the item is used a lot; you have multiple users of an item, and the item is mobile.

I personally purchased a warranty for 2 years on a laptop for my 12 year-old son. About a year later, he somehow, some way, blew the motherboard out. I took the laptop and warranty back to the store. The customer service representative took the laptop to the repair section. The laptop was accepted, worked on, and returned to my son free of charge. Phew, I am so glad that I didn't have to spend another $399 on a replacement laptop. My son used that computer for a total of 4 years, and then we upgraded to a new laptop just this past year.

I have extended warranties on all of my major purchases like my washer, dryer, stove, computers, and televisions. I keep all of my warranties in a large plastic envelope in a safe place. I have particular warranties that allow for my major appliances to have an annual maintenance service for free. For me, warranties are well worth the investment.

IV. Invest

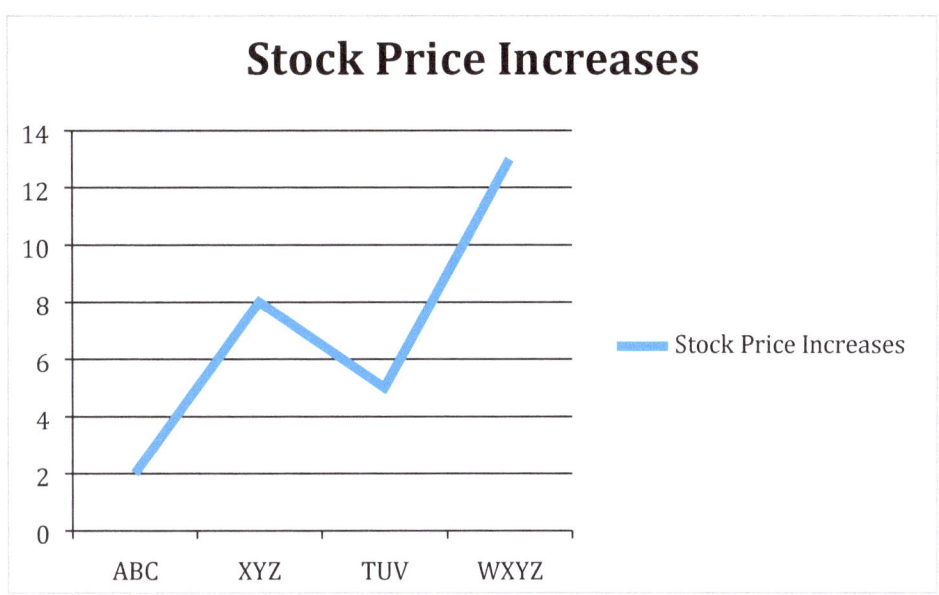

Chapter 10
Investing Ideas

You need to set aside another 10% of your income to invest each month. Why? Investing can allow your money to grow at a faster percent than just putting you money into a savings account or a money market checking account.

If you are new to investing, I would recommend you seek the assistance of a professional financial advisor or a money manager. These professionals can assist you in determining which investments are best for you.

I will share some tips about basic investments. These <mark>basic investments</mark> include stocks, mutual funds, bonds, real estate, and even a college education.

Stocks

If you are buying stocks on your own or with a money manager, you must open an account with a brokerage. Your money manager/ financial advisor will assist you in opening an investment account. A ==brokerage== is a person or a firm that charges commission or a fee for executing buy and sell orders submitted by an investor.

When you buy ==stocks==, you are buying ownership shares in a company or corporation. The goal of buying stocks is to buy them when the price is low and sell them when the price is high so that you can make a nice profit.

If you are able, you also want to diversify your stock investments. For example, in May a person may want to purchase 10 shares of a technology company that has stocks priced at $20 a share. The person will pay 10 x $20= $200 + $25(an estimated brokerage commission fee) which equals $225.

In June the same person may want to buy 20 shares in a food corporation priced at $15 a share. The price for the 20 shares will be $325, 20 x $15= $300 + $25 (commission) = $325.

I always suggest that even if you are working with a professional, you should research the companies you are interested in buying stock in. Sometimes it may take years for some stocks to grow. Therefore, you must be patient in the short term and ride the stock's up and down waves for the long term. Good news about a company or corporation can send a stock's price soaring; just as bad news can send the stock's price lower. When a stock's price is lower than what you paid for it and you know the company is still in good standing, you have the option to hold on to it and not sell it. However, if the company is not doing well at all, and the stock's price is sliding down hill quickly, you have the option of selling the stock before you lose most or all of the money you invested in the stock. The best idea would be to seek professional advice on whether to buy or sell your stocks.

Mutual Funds

A mutual fund is an investment instrument that contains many, possibly even hundreds of individual stocks or bonds. It usually has a fund manager that determines which investments the fund will sell, buy, or hold. A great benefit of owning mutual funds is that even if you have a limited amount of money mutual funds are automatically diversified with different stocks or bonds. A mutual fund has a buffering if one of the particular stocks doesn't do as well. Otherwise, with stocks, you absorb the loss because it is a single investment.

No-load mutual funds are a good type of mutual fund to invest in because it has no sales commission when you buy and sell the mutual fund. However, you need to check to see if the no-load mutual fund has a low yearly expense ratio. High annual expense ratios will decrease your returns.

Bonds are a means for corporations and governments to borrow money. Yes, you are lending the corporation and/or government money for a certain period of time. The money that you lend to them is called principal. The issuer of the bond will pay interest on the amount of the money you loaned them until the bond matures. When a bond matures, it can be cashed, and the principal plus interest are returned to you.

Real Estate

Many people love to invest in real estate. There are shows on TV that make it look so easy to renovate, flip, and/or rent properties.

If you can successfully buy a property in your market area at a low price and flip it for a profit, then you will do well with flipping homes. Some people enjoy purchasing properties and renting them out for monthly income. Other people like to purchase commercial properties and rent them to businesses.

Here are some things to consider if you chose to invest in real estate. You will need to have a network of professionals and companies such as a real estate agent, good credit for a mortgage or proof of funds in order to purchase a property, an inspector, insurance agent, a title company, appraiser, a plumber, and a real estate attorney. You will also need a good, trustworthy contractor if you are not remodeling or improving the property yourself.

If you choose to invest in real estate, make sure you check with your municipal building inspector to apply for permits before beginning any remodeling projects. You may also want to review the county or municipal rules for the area in which you are leasing a home or apartment to a renter.

If you are leasing a commercial building to other businesses, you will need to check with the municipality's zoning and code offices to determine what kinds of businesses can conduct business in your commercial building.

When investing in real estate, you may consider joining a real estate investment group or club where you can find a mentor to help you with your real estate investment goals. Always remember; it may be expensive, but you can consult a real estate attorney to aid you in reaching your goals as well.

A College Education

A college education is a major investment that may potentially pay itself off in the long run. This is possible if you don't accumulate too much student loan debt and select a lucrative career.

Here are some ways to cut the costs of college. You want to start planning as early as possible. Many people create college savings plans for infants. However, if you have no savings plan for college, it is time to start. Some people open a savings account to deposit monetary gifts and income from part time jobs. Some utilize a financial advisor to invest their college savings money in investments where it can accrue interest. No matter which approach you take, do not touch or make withdrawals from your college savings account. That would defeat the purpose of saving.

Make sure you complete and submit all federal and state financial aid forms before their deadlines. Conduct scholarship searches online and contact local businesses, social organizations, churches, and agencies to inquire if they provide scholarships.

Have a yard sale or start selling old and no longer used items like video games, DVDs, and game consoles. Selling these items may bring in a few dollars to help with college expenses.

Most importantly, if your parents are taking out or cosigning a loan on your behalf, they need to obtain an insurance policy on you for the amount of that loan. It is a sad reality, but if you should pass away before the loan is paid in full, your parents may possibly be still responsible for repayment of the loan. Closely check your loan terms to see what it states in writing about repayment due to the untimely passing of a student.

V. Donate

Chapter 11
Tithe and Donate to Good Causes

The old adage "It's better to give than to receive," has some merit. Think about it. If you are able to give to others who are in need, then you have abundance on your side.

Always donate to 501(c) 3 organizations no matter if it is religious or not. A 501(c) 3 organization is a tax-exempt, nonprofit. When you donate to a 501(c) 3 organization, your donations are tax deductible.

Pay your tithe! What's a tithe? It's when you give a tenth of your income as a donation to 501(c) 3 non-profit, religious organizations that you belong to. The tithe is great for a non-profit organization because it provides support for its programming and pays its monthly bills. Your tithe donations are tax deductible.

There are thousands of 501(c) 3 organizations out there that are not religious in their origin. Before donating to any one that is unfamiliar to you, you may want to investigate their website and visit the organization and inquire about how your donations will be used.

Once you donate to any non-profit organization, keep your receipts in a file. This will make the task of organizing receipts for tax time much easier.

By reading this book, you have gained knowledge on how to manage your money wisely. Stay focused and remain aware that it may be tempting to fall back into your old money management ways. However, it is now time for you to apply the new knowledge you have learned by earning an income, saving, spending wisely, investing, and donating your money with common sense.

VI. Appendix

Monthly Budget for Young Adults

Name of Bills	Payment Amount	Due Date	Comments
Rent or Mortgage			
Electric			
Gas			
Cell &/or Home Phone			
Water/Sewer			
Cable or Satellite TV			
Food & Lunches			
Medicine			
Entertainment			
Gas/Bus Pass/Jitney/Ride Share Fees			
Child Care			
Clothing			
Insurance (auto, home/renters, life, health)			
Credit Card or Charge Accounts			
1.			
2.			
3.			
4.			
Loan Payments			
1.			
2.			
3.			
Church/Charity Donations			
Miscellaneous/Unexpected			
Savings			
Investments			
Total Expenses Per Month			
Actual Take Home Pay Per Month			
Subtract Total Expenses from Actual Take Home Pay = Net (what you have left over). Fill Net in the first gray box below.	$ -$_____ Net=		
The goal is to have some money left over.			

Monthly Budget for Teenagers

Name of Bills	Payment Amount	Due Date	Comments
Cell Phone			
Snacks			
Entertainment (Dates, DVD Rentals)			
Gas/Bus Pass			
Church/Charity			
Miscellaneous Unexpected			
Savings			
Total Expenses Per Month			
Total Actual Take Home Pay or Allowance			
Subtract Total Expenses from Actual Take Home Pay or Allowance to get the Net of what you have left over. Fill Net in the first box gray below.	$ -$_____ Net=		
The goal is to have some money left over.			

VII. Acknowledgements

I would sincerely like to acknowledge my mom, Peggy; my sons, Lloyd Jr., Calvin, and Kyle; my cousin, Jane; my friend, Kellie M., and anyone else who has inspired me to write this book. It was your encouragement and support that made the completion of this book possible.

Notes